Walking Natural Pathways

by

Mark A. Doherty

Published by Unsolicited Press
www.unsolicitedpress.com

Copyright © Mark A. Doherty 2018

All Rights Reserved.

No part of this book may be reproduced or transmitted in any form or by any means without written permission from the publisher or author.

For information, contact the publisher at info@unsolicitedpress.com

Unsolicited Press Books are distributed to the trade by Ingram. Printed in the United States of America.
ISBN: 978-1-947021-41-9

For Deborah

whose first love was the mountains

Contents

Part 1 Diverse Views 1
    The Stone 2
    Polished Rock 3
    The Boy and the Bear 4
    Predator 6
    Whisker 8
    Goodbye 9
    Snow Silence 11
    Lemming 12
    Henry, John, Teddy, Aldo, Ed and Me 13
    Cancerous Nature 16

Part 2 Extended Seasons and Reasons 17
    Political Climate at the Water Cooler 18
    Water Commissioner 21
    Colorado Wild 22
    The Blood of our Mother 25

Part 3 Vignettes and Images 27
    Alpine Thaw 28
    Bristlecone-The Watching Sentinel 30
        I. 27
        II. 30
        III. 31

IV. 31

   Crossroads of the Winds 30

   Finding Moments Amidst 35

   The Wood Pile 37

   Some Journeys 39

   The Gifts Invisible 41

   Seeds and Roots 43

   Winter Flood 44

   Wingtip Wisdom 46

Part 4 Seasonal Sonnets 48

   Winter's First, A Month Away 49

   Winter's Nocturn 50

   Springsong Sonnet 51

   Summerfull 52

   Autumnways 53

   Equinox 54

   December's Song 55

Part 5 Lyrical Songs 56

   Whitewater Eyes 57

   Moenkopi Memories 59

   Fire in the Sky 60

   Wilderness Save Us (Direct Our Evolution) 61

   Great Massive Stone in the River 62

Hand Made Time	63
Ponderosa Sing to Me	64
Gold and Wood	65
Song for the Burr Trail	61
From the Mountains Down	62
Mountain Goats	63
Ranger's Call	64
Summits That He Climbed	66
Heart of the Desert	74
Old Dusty Road	75
I Am The Wind	76
Seasons Are Changin'	78
Drinkin' From a Glass	79
Last Night the Old Arch Tumbled Down	80
Save The Canyon Wilderness	82
Carry Me Across The Canyon	83
About the Author	84

Part 1

Diverse Views

The Stone

Small and round—
storm-polished,
it shines in sun
and glistens in rain.
Weather and wind have
worn rough edges away,
seam lines and hues to
reveal its mineral origins.

Polished Rock

If you roll me round in the palm of your hand,
I no longer grate and scrape like I used to.
The storms of worry and seasons of struggle,
the freeze and thaw of rage to realization,
have worn away my rough edges.
Yet I've retained the lines and colors that shape my roots.

If you could crack me open,
you would see the intricate crystals of
imagination, thought, and experience
binding me, holding me together.
Perhaps someday I'll be polished smooth
 like granite over the grave.
How sad it would be for you to feel nothing
of the grains that mix and twist and turn within me.

The Boy and the Bear

Frantic, running feet scuffing the surface
of hard-packed rural dirt road
are the only other sound he hears—
aside from perhaps blood pounding
through quick breathing, and ringing, ears.

Growl of great bear
rises from the starry darkness
of mountain summer night.
Legs find their way over the bumpy
gravel road—eternal forested quarter mile
to home—leaving imagination
free to anticipate
claws reaching from behind,
ravenous red mouth—
teeth that shine like slivers of new moon
dripping with saliva
at the thought of tasting
a young boy's blood.

A distant glimmer of home
gives breath to wheezing lungs—
He lunges, in bounds, up the steep driveway
And slams into home.

Soon the sound is precisely recounted—
Father listens,
the boy's heart rate calms.

"Why, Son, have you never heard
the nighthawk dive to catch the moth?
That roar of wings

is alarming when they swoop
so close to your ears!"

Predator

Grizzly, standing, surveys the clearing
amidst brushy undergrowth
where virgin timber sways in mountain storm,
and ungulates roam the paths
through forest floors with splashing brooks.
The cubs have come to learn.

Wolf, wandering wild, keeps the lonely vigil
atop the bluff below high peaks
where tundra rolls into river,
and caribou migrate in meanders
toward green fertility of spring.
The pack will soon arrive.

Mountain Lion, staring, statuesque, maintains watch
upon the granite between trees
where scrub oak and juniper rise onto the plateau,
and elk graze in meadow herds
along sage openings to aspen.
The pride must now awake.

Golden Eagle rises on cumulus cloud thermals
above wild mesas and mountains and canyons
where grasses and shrubs carpet the clearings,
and myriad creatures wander hummocks
amidst meadow, glen and alcove.
A mate's piercing cry precipitates a dive.

Man, stands in the bed, of his pickup truck
along the ragged dirt track scar
where erosion gullies create gulches
and distant lights twinkle glaringly on endless horizons

across plain, valley, riverbank, and seashore.
A brass-encased round clicks – mechanical.

Whisker

Brushes on bare leg
with featherstroke tickling,
firmly passing judgment—
The cat is saying hello.

Springs resiliently as
wire-thin sensory flexes
forward catching pheromone motion
and cool calculated shifts in the winds
laden with moisture, or musk, or miniscule insects
clinging to the camouflage of grass—
The cat passes, silently sensing.

Lingers before prey
quivering with precise tension
and predatory predilection
that fascinates the child
who draws first the
thin lines followed by
   two triangles
  for   ears.

Goodbye

The old man, Forrest,
squeezed her hand
and said, finally, "There were good
days, and bad days,
but I'm just glad that there were
so many days."
Welling with tears,
her eyes watched his hand in hers—
she, his caretaker says finally,
"Relax, rest, go still."

The aged cat Tiger
purred in his master's lap
and squinted his nearly blind eyes
With satisfaction as if to say,
"I feel your palms,
they are always so warm and welcome
on my chilled, stiffening muscles."
Trembling with acceptance,
his hand felt the soft striped paw
release, rest, fall away.

The hospitalized mother Melanie
reached for her children
and whispered,
"Be strong, make Father proud,
and know that I'll be looking out for you
from the place I now must go."
Twisting with self-control
their faces observed
her chest fall to stillness.

The cherished companion Jerry
gazed into his lover's eyes
and spoke to his partner,
"It was only society,
never we,
who was wrong."
Bowing in acquiescence,
he waited for the monitor
to summon a steady, final tone.

The crimson leaf maple
rustled on the highest limb
and felt the cold sleet saying,
"Fall with me now,
for winter
is beckoning us all."
Standing in solemn relief,
the tree fell silent
within the sleep of snow.

Snow Silence

Listen to the silence
Of the winter's song—
All the geese have flown
And the last dry leaves
Clicking on bare limbs
Have clattered to the ground—
Fallen.

Low sun lights the quiet stage
As stillness closes in with night.
Curtained stars settle around
To mark the end of day.

Yet deep within
Stillness of winter
Subtle voices can be heard,
Like the snowflake's falling sound.
It simply takes more listening
To hear winter's
Silent song.

Lemming

Use it up
Because
That's the master plan—
Man
Is destined biologically
To be the agent of ultimate change:
      Extinction

Must occur before
Rebirth
Of a new earth
Somewhere else
In the broad universe
Where minerals, moisture, and
That essence called life
Will gather energy that is never lost—
Energy that merely moves
In an opposite and equal direction—
And create new life
Once again.

Henry, John, Teddy, Aldo, Ed and Me

Henry,
 I'm glad you are not here to see
the algae blooms and bacterial notices
posted on the trees between the posh
homes that adorn the wooded shores of your pond.
Rumpled-skin retirees in speedos
lounge in the literary afterglow
with their books face down
next to their martinis resting on
the wide arms of sun chairs.
> I have but to read one chapter
> of *Walden* to be with you, then,
> philosophizing in your quiet presence.

John,
You are lucky not to see
the traffic jams at the gates
next to the antlike swarms
spilling from campground to creek
and clinging to the cliffs
like so many spiders
emerging from the woods
in floods of grass-trampling feet.
> I have but to turn a few pages
> of your essays on Yosemite
> to exercise with you in your pristine exuberance.

Teddy,
You are fortunate not to hear
the rifle shots taking the last grizzly
and the last wolf
from the contiguous forty-eight

where cars roam like mad cows
through a stockyard of subdivisions
glowing eternally with electric light.
    I have but to recall your portraits
    and words of political passion
    to be that American moved to save just a little.

Aldo,
I'm happy not to report
the journey of the last old growth
as it makes its way on massive barges
down the great rivers
and across the oceans
to foreign countries
leaving behind the churned soil
of clear cut slopes
that will only produce a distant memory
of the grandeur that once stood.
    I have but to return to your *Almanac*
    discussing the great trees
    to wonder at ecology's complexities.

Edward,
I'm so relieved
in an anal sort of way
not to have you see
the great sinkholes that mark
the result of westward expansion
and Las Vegas style water waste.
You were right when you claimed that
only an economy that expands or expires
Is false to all that is human.
    As I turn the pages

> of *Desert Solitaire* I return
> to a piercing view of environment.

As for me,
I sit in the tiny garden of a national park,
using writings as time machines
to transport me to a wilder America
that made us all strong.
Beyond the buffer that seems no more than
a thin wall surrounding a tiny plot,
I cannot help but hear the sounds
of the city progressing ever closer.
> Yet I draw comfort from the sight
> of the weeds whose roots are prying
> the cracks in sidewalk cement
> on their eternal quest
> to reclaim all that was once lost.

Cancerous Nature

The brain which attempts to control its body Earth is now riddled with cancerous growth, evidenced by splotches spread like clear-cut rashes over once virgin skin, seen in stagnant, poisoned pockets of the sea of cells flowing in bloodstream rivers. Even symbiotic organisms, consumed by expanding fermentation, leave irruption of species boils and storm swells and insect cists to blemish. Inexorable, the brain expands, slowly warming to accommodate for critical masses consuming the air, the water, the fuel, the food. Undoubtedly a few fragments of original organism will remain after cancer completes its course, and beneath biospheric cataclysms of death perhaps a new eusocial species, a new brain will someday evolve.

Part 2

Extended Seasons and Reasons

Political Climate at the Water Cooler

My grandfather started this company.
My dad and all his brothers
built their lives—families, homes, careers—
by working the fields, driving the trucks,
managing the refineries, and eventually directing stocks.
We have always taken pride in providing
the most essential resource our country will ever need.
Here, have a cup.
This cooler really filters the crap out.

So how can a few granola-eating
tea-drinking ocean kayakers
have the audacity to claim the coast is theirs to protect—
These people who drive gasoline powered
cars and travel in oil fueled jets
staying in energy-heated resorts
playing on their electronic devices
transported by diesel powered barge from China—
these people who claim that drilling and pipelines
are ruining their world.
Let me get a refill.
I need to take my medication.

Don't they realize that we *made* their world?
Don't they know that my family's legacy
provided the fuel for the ships
and planes that have protected America
from the scourges of earth since World War I?
Even their clothes, modern high-tech
synthetics, super light and weatherproof
are made from the product of
my family's labors and business acumen.

Excuse me.
Let me toss this cup into the trash behind you.

I simply cannot believe that some senators
deign to listen
to such rubbish that claims
progress is causing the climate to change!
The climate is *always* changing, always has,
always will.
Only through progress—the kind of progress
my family has created—
will humankind to survive those natural
swings in weather and storm
that would wipe out a simple-minded culture,
like the culture the average environmentalist wants.
It's technology, and the fuel that saves us,
that will keep America strong.
Umm, that pill didn't go down so well,
Give me another cup.

And then they start arguing about
the national parks and public lands.
Why, if they had their way
oil production would grind to a halt
and we'd all be walking to work,
and every home in the northern states
would freeze solid in winter
and melt down in summer.
You know, those national parks were originally
established as *resources* for America.
You know what we should do?
We should just give them a few states
and let them go live there

without any oil, without any electricity.
See how long they survive!
Maybe California, Oregon, and Washington—
but not Alaska, we've got too much
invested there—
Once they're all gone and settled
in their environmentalist paradise
we can get back to work
making progress, making the world
comfortable and prosperous.
Will you toss this cup in the trash for me?
Thanks.

Well, enough of this,
I think you get my drift.
Excuse me now while I make a few calls,
Election time is coming
And I've got some money to spend.

Water Commissioner

My field work
is filled with fountain sounds
of Parshall Flumes,
where weirs channel
liquid gold past
stream gages with
chart houses,
cubic feet per second,
and Stevens Recorders
that read the flow
like stockbrokers cataloguing
the ups and downs of Wall Street.

My water world
is adjudicated by laws
of prior appropriation
and acre feet of generations
that were fought for and won
by shovel and rifle,
ditch and decision.
Streamflow, replacement volumes,
water rights and wells
define my existence, my job.

And I have the power
to turn the cast iron wheel
and close the headgate down.
My diversion control can shrivel a farm
or parch a town.
So I say, conserve—
don't make me turn you off.

Colorado Wild

It was the wettest spring on record
And the spring storm alpine rain was melting snow,
With the churning muddy waters
Even the biggest dam was on the verge.

We set out on the river
The morning that the dam was topping high,
With outlets pouring maximum,
Like wind down the canyon we did fly.

Every little wash,
Every waterfall was spring storm full,
And as the gray clouds darkly deepened,
We were ever aware of the river's pull.

Three days down the river,
In a spot that other times would take us ten,
We made a high ledge camp twenty feet above the water,
Wondering if the rain would ever end.

To boulders crashing in the morning
We woke with our boats now only feet below,
And wondered at the awesome waves
Of a river running completely out of control.

Then a chopper in the canyon hovered over,
A crying speaker echoed from the walls,
"Stand by for a rescue, river's gone too wild.
Canyon is now closed to one and all!"

    Colorado River of mighty energy
    Run wild and free, like the river you used to be.

But before they could return
We packed and strapped our gear,
Heartbeats pounding iron in our brains,
And set out on the wild river in the rain!

A hundred miles above
With a billion tons behind,
The rotted, sandstone walls were giving way.
The concrete monster would soon take its final sway.
We moored one more night tucked tightly
In the crevice of a high side canyon wall
With someone awake and waiting
To watch, to listen, and to call.

With the dawn came the rumble,
We barely reached the main current line
Before the river surged a hundred feet
In only five short minutes of time.

> Colorado River of mighty energy
> Run wild and free, like the river you used to be.
> Take the bridges and the dams
> And grind them into sand, run wild, run free.

So little I remember of flying through the canyons
Using every wit to stay alive,
Waves as big as mountains
Crumbling shorelines just a blur as we swept by.

We didn't stop at Hoover, Parker, or even Davis,
All were gaping holes as we sailed by.
Evening found us not a hundred miles from Mexico
Beneath the windy stars of a clearing sky.

When we reached the ocean, most our gear was gone,
But we'd made it through, two boats and seven lives,
And we'd seen the world changing, seen a new age coming,
On the Colorado River running free, and running wild.

The Blood of our Mother

The blood of our Mother
Flows cold from the land
Where trees are uprooted
And torn down by man.

Her soft skin now glistens
With uncovered wounds,
She calls us to listen,
We must stop soon.

She bleeds as the trees
Fall to the chains,
She cries as the skies
Pour acid rains,
She weeps as the seas
Are blackened again.

The milk of our Mother
Is poisoned and stale
As wild rivers surrender
And fresh waters fail.

Her blue skies are troubled
You can see the pain,
To use her and waste her
Is a most deadly game.

Part 3

Vignettes and Images

Alpine Thaw

Smells of cool spring air filter
through frigid stones.
Sun rises,
as old winter snow
gleams and refracts
spiny crystals of evening ice.

Silence of dawn hours,
then softens to sounds of watery rivulets
from newly melted snow
growing louder through clear air.
Audible becomes thawing streams,
little falls, and slumping snow.
Sun rises higher.

Ice cracks beside steaming rocks as
bits of snow, falling freely from cornice,
float past heated cliff,
shining, spinning.
Plunging onto fields of white below
and slide smoothly,
leaving a clean glimmering trail behind
in the dusty old snow.

Now larger chunks, the entire cornice front,
crashes over the shining wet cliffs
churning into the snow beneath.
And the snowfield surface layer slides,
down past stray boulders
with stone and snow alike
rumbling to the lake below.

Suddenly the wet avalanche slows, and ends.
It leaves a spotless white trail,
lapped at end
by the waters of the icy jaded tarn.
Miles below, the timberline sighs
and drinks deeply of earth and air.
Sun sets last upon the peak,
while jagged edge of the cornice,
now half its size,
hardens as the trickles cease.

Landscape halts its alpine motion.
A white haze forms over the emerald pool,
and the snow colors pink
with quickly fading alpenglow.
A glimmer of grayish white and dark, then dusk.
Smells of the cool spring air filters through
wintered stones.

Bristlecone-The Watching Sentinel

I.
Standing majestically
On the precipitous edge
Of the granite canyon,
The great Bristlecone pine
Weathers the passing years
Like a sentinel,
Guarding the passages
Hidden in the cliffs below
Which lead far into
The mysterious heart
Of the sleeping mountains.

II.
High and Alone
I stand on the mountain
High up and alone,
Bent, ancient, and twisted;
I'm the old Bristlecone.

When Odysseus sailed
On his quest from his shore,
Or when chariots clashed
In Caesar's great war,
I was here on the mountain
With limbs reaching high,
And I'd already seen
A thousand years passing by.

I've seen the great forests,
Both rise and then decline,

As they built castles, cathedrals,
And cities through time.
Great fires and blight
Have consumed other trees,
While I clung to this mountain
In the high rocky breeze.

Now tenacious in old age
I am filled with surprise
To see stewards of forests
Begin to arise.

III.
Imagine a tree
Living high and alone,
Twisted with age,
Knarled by storm,
Ancient yet growing—
It's the old Bristlecone.
Four thousand years
It has stood thriving strong;
There is little on earth
That has survived so long.
August and imposing,
Worthy of poems
Worthy of song
Bristlecone pine
So old, yet so fine.

IV.
I stand on the mountain,
High up and alone,
Bent, ancient, and twisted;
I'm the old Bristlecone.

When Odysseus sailed
On his quest from his shore,
Or when chariots clashed
In Caesar's great war,

I was here on the mountain
Etching the sky,
And I'd already seen
A thousand years pass by.

Now I'm four thousand,
And what is in store?
Someday, like all things,
I'll stand here no more.

Crossroads of the Winds

Standing at the crossroads
Of the winds
Atop this airy summit,
We can see pathways
Of the winter's white snows
Flowing in all directions
From the cirques
To the forested valleys below.
We have but to listen,
To breathe God's wisdom
In the rarified air.
We have but to see,
To dream the beauty
Long after we've departed.
We have but to feel,
To beat our hearts in rhythm
With the wild creatures
That climb and soar.

When we do this,
Our course will carry us
Like waters flowing, falling
Safely through the cascades
And into the deep lakes of wisdom
That reflect always
The mountains and the stars.

Your crossroads are now
Clear as a crisp summit
In the morning sun.
May you always bask
In this moment of lucid light.

We must always remember
As we descend from the summits, that
Evanescence merely opens the window
For a new dawn.

Finding Moments Amidst

In the winter we find
The hidden rainbows
Of sunlight divided
Where they cast their
Magical light into the deepest
Corners of the darkness.
In the summer we happen upon
The speckled comfort
Of cool breeze shade
Where it drapes its
Soothing darkness upon the searing
Vast plains of bright hot light.

In the world wild with
Demands and unconscious souls
Striving for senseless destinations
We seek moments of solace,
And wiser ways from older times
Which will guide us into calm
When the seas of society wreak havoc.

Our failures are our stepping stones
Into a universe that exists
Within, yet beyond, daily
Human existence.
Our successes are the moments
Of surcease that enable us to
See beyond—
Know without doubt
That there are no regrets
On the pathways we follow.

We need not look back,
Only forward into the horizon
Where the stones of our trail
Appear within reach
One at a time.
And places to rest and admire the view
Are heavenly.

The Wood Pile

I gaze at the neatly stacked wood pile,
Each piece fits the spaces—
A mathematical rhythm in time,
Marking the magic of seasons.

In spring we are burning the last
Dredges of winter—twigs
And remnants of wood.
The cocoons of praying mantis
Left undisturbed
Are set aside for summer's garden.
We shake away the widow
And let her be on her way,
While the damp chips and bark
Sizzle and smoke.

In summer as we hike
We plan the woodpile
To include last season's deadfall
And note the opportunity
For autumn's wood harvest.

By fall the pile has long since
Been carefully planned and placed
With loads of freshly split
Pieces tossed from hand to hand
Added dearly to the pile
As family and friends
Build aromatic memories
In the lingering sun and sawdust.

Then winter arrives—

We admire the artistic wood pile,
Each piece stacked carefully,
Each piece in its place.
It represents reminiscence,
Accomplishment, warmth and
The comfort of home.

Sometimes deep into the season
As we gather an armload
For the warm fire inside,
Someone long gone, for a fleeting moment
Hands us the last piece
And our arms are full.

May warmth and good memories
Kindle the fire of your hearts.

Some Journeys

Some journeys begin
Like a great expedition
Where we are dropped
With nothing but experience
And a little camping gear
Deep in the wilderness
From which we hope
To emerge renewed,
Refreshed, rejuvenated
And perhaps even enlightened.

Some journeys
Go awry, even moments after
The bush plane departs.
One can still hear the distant
Hum of security
Slowly dissipating
Into the vast horizon.

Some journeys
Cost dearly, exacting
Great tolls.
Sometimes they take our strength,
Sometimes they take our resources,
But never have they taken our lives.
We are too strong for that,
Too determined,
Too aware,
And tuned in
To divine guidance.

Some journeys leave us

On the brink—
Before we find the stars
To guide us back,
Before we realize the constellation
Within our hearts
Can give us bearings,
Can bring us safely home.

On this Valentine's Eve my dear
I look forward to the hour
When we can drink a toast
Somewhere Home
And say,
That was
Some Journey.

The Gifts Invisible

Again we graciously lift
Meaningful mementoes—
An arrowhead, a tomahawk,
A stone knife—
From inside treaded tracks left
By unconscious humanity—
Some soul ran blindly,
Drove deliriously,
Tearing soft fragile soil.
But they motored right over

Culture, oblivious to it,
Leaving the essence of spare desert fabric
Intact, unchanged, waiting
For the inspired hand to grasp it.

Again we intuitively trace
Ethereal emanations—
A ghostly pictograph, a fading petroglyph,
A smoke streaked stain—
Beneath angry scrawls left
By effacing humanity—
Some soul scraped hurriedly,
Marring the surface.
But they wrote on top of
Culture, oblivious to it,
While the old message though worn still speaks,
Intact, unchanged, waiting
For the enlightened eye to see it.

Again we consciously gesture
Altruistic alternatives—

The bicycle, the cross-country ski,
The small sail, the kayak—
Amidst the chaotic din
Of blindly indoctrinated humanity—
Most souls drink poisonously,
Fouling their own lives—
They continually storm past
Culture, oblivious to it,
While those few illuminated keep their vigil,
Sanguine, unchanged, waiting
For the spirited voice, at the precise moment,
To speak it.

Seeds and Roots

Your joy in finding
And perceiving the simple
Unseen things in life—
Your smiles that come
Despite difficult days
And impossible people—
Your quick wit
That leaves most people
In dazed wonder—
Your brilliant nuances
Of language so clever
They are hard to phantom—
Your gently moving
Dance when we
Walk together—
Your ability to find light
During the darkest days
Of Winter—
Your willingness to travel
The paths of interstice
Where life slows—

All of these things nourish my love for you,
Keeping the flame of our passion alive,
Always planting new seeds, feeding new roots
So that we may often travel from Winter Solstice
To spring,
Where we feel eternally young,
And forever in love.

Winter Flood

The cold black water
Applauds, distantly subdued,
And gurgles in places
Beneath the ice
As it meanders through
The rusts, greys,
Blacks and snow-covered whites
Of the tiny little state park
Nature preserve near home.
Cottonwood, willow, dogwood, aspen,
Sage and tall grasses
All adorn the banks, all leafless
And dormant and brittle
In the dry cold of winter.
And often the slick waters
Disappear beneath the white
Or sometimes blue-gray ice.

But one winter day
Loud violence rent asunder
The murmuring silence and stillness—
For a flood released upstream
And came hissing and grinding
Into the sanctuary
Like an angry bull
In a glass house.
Slices of ice the size of wall panels
Jaggedly upended and rolled
Amidst the newly browned muddy torrent,
And a pungent scent of rich wet earth and soil
Assaulted the wintry air.
A standing four foot wave

Of brown water, driftwood, and massive ice chunks
Grumbled beneath the footbridge
As the flood surged
Into the reservoir below.
The ground vibrated, then stilled
As the waters abated.

Soon new snows covered the muddied banks,
Ice again encased portions of the stream,
And the water slowed, and cleared
Like black obsidian.

But for weeks,
Tabletops of six-inch ice
Lay far up the river banks,
Evaporating in the dry winter sun.

The cause?
Still and unknown
Lurking upstream
Somewhere in the dark
Of winter's mystery.

Wingtip Wisdom

I love to see you spread your wings
And soar above the earth,
As if you were born to fly
From the moment of your birth.

I watch you turn upon the winds
And spiral through thermals high,
As if you know to use each cloud
Before it passes by.

I fly with you a wingtip close
And reach out for the sun,
As if the place we're meant to be
Is where great deeds are done.

The diamond sun shines on the snow
And on the blue green waves,
And in your eyes reflects the light
Of wise and knowing ways.

The crystal glass tips to the taste
And toasts to our love,
As our spirits soar on wings
And guard us from above.

Part 4

Seasonal Sonnets

Winter's First, A Month Away

Onward through the fading light we go,
Not sure we are prepared for days to come.
These winter nights deep frosted with white snow
Have made us wistful, longing for the sun.
And yet the season's cold has just commenced
Now to grasp us in its icy chills,
Keep summer dreams now gone so far distanced—
Safe locked beyond the leagues of whitened hills.
Gone to the earth, leaves, flowers, butterflies
Instead the slush and snow drifts cold and wet.
Voluminous the clouds occlude the skies,
Icing the sun even more coldly yet.
Next month, however, the Winter Solstice means
Growing light, for six months, more sunbeams!

Winter's Nocturn

When angles of the sun are shining low,
Intuition tells us we must sleep.
Nocturnal tracks appear now in the snow
To mark the chilly vigil some must keep.
Enlightened constellations rule the skies,
Reminding us that distant worlds must be,
So vast the universe, so short our eyes.
Omniscience sets imagination free.
Light festivals will keep us from the dark,
So long the nights, so chilly and so cold.
The landscape seems now barren and now stark
In spite of seeds of summer that it holds.
Cold winter's night now turns the other way—
Envisions six months hence the longest day.

Springsong Sonnet

Sublime are changes deep within the ground,
Presenting tips of green thought bulging earth,
Releasing buds with flowers all around,
Incensed air saturated with rebirth.
Now reaching skyward buds adorn the trees,
Great rushing sap will rise within each arm
In time to burst alive with new green laves
Suffused with light, such iridescent charm.
Come back all creatures who've been six months gone,
Or hibernated long within cocoons,
My garden anxiously awaits your song,
In melodies of green, I'll revel soon.
Now spring's first day has dawned its balanced sun,
Go breathe and sing and laugh and stretch and run.

Summerfull

So much effulgence greets the wandering eyes,
Unveiling life, which burgeons form the trees.
Meandering with the sounds and scents that rise
Midway between the breaths of morning's breeze.
Each moment seems to stretch the endless day,
Revolving to the ever-present sun,
So does the solstice subtly slip away
On golden stems where harvests' snow begun.
Like magic floating on the fragrant air,
Sublimity of ease beneath warm skies
Takes all old struggles, all the wintry cares
Into green fields, to let them free and fly.
Come to the feast, it' time to celebrate
Each moment, from this dawn, to dusk so late.

Autumnways

As life moves westward to the seasons set,
Unspoken forces ripen fruits and seeds
Toward the harvest, while the sun is yet
Upholding warmth fulfilling summer's needs.
My thoughts become more pensive and serene,
Nighttime chills make sweaters feel secure—
So warm the sunny days, so cool between
Halfway to winter's night it seems so near.
And in the predawn chill Orion's rise
Ret8urning to a differing view of space
Verifies the move toward winter skies
Evolving slowly into summer's place.
So subtly moving seasons bring the change
To where the natural circles rearrange.

Equinox

As autumn's changes move across the days
Unveiling colors like the turning page
To guide the movements upon nature's stage,
Upon which movements of the season play,
More deeply does our heart's emotion flow
Next to sublime within the psyche's eyes
Into the realm of clouds and changing skies.
So subtly, the approaching season grows.
Cool and frost begin to nip the nose
Or freeze the puddles left by autumn rains.
My breath now steams with every great exhale—
Inside the fire burning warms my toes.
Nostalgia lingers for the sunny lanes—
Go breathe once more before the warm light fails.

December's Song

Come wintry gloom the celebrating time
Has made the season seems less dark and gray.
Remembering that December's gift sublime
Is marked by solstice, winter's turning day.
So festive lights and garlands will adorn
The latent corners of each snow-filled yard,
Mix colorful and bright from dusk to morn,
And make the chill of winter seems less hard.
Sometimes we join in feasting and in song—
Comradery that brings the evenings cheer
Has power to sustain the nights so long—
Endearing memories lasting through the years.
Each one of us will find a smile to share,
Revealing kindness hope, and love, and care.

Part 5

Lyrical Songs

Whitewater Eyes

This mornin' she's a river running free,
Tomorrow she'll be looking to the sea,
This evenin' listen closely to the breeze,
Hear her sing a canyon mystery.

This morning she's the water passing by,
Tonight her eyes will shine in a starry sky,
Tomorrow she'll be gone a hundred miles,
Leaving nothing but the memory of her smile.

>   A lover in the springtime, whitewater eyes,
>   A lullaby in autumn, bright clear blue skies,
>   From snowfall on mountaintops to canyons below,
>   The river flows.

This mornin' she's an eagle flyin' high,
Tomorrow she'll be on the mountain side,
This evening see the full moon in the night,
Hear the treetops rustle as she sighs.

This mornin' she's white summer fields of snow,
Tonight she'll freeze again within the cold,
Tomorrow into streams she'll melt and flow,
Leaving alpine grasses where the flowers grow,

>   Full passion in the springtime, whitewater eyes,
>   Gentleness in autumn, bright clear blue skies,
>   From snowfall on mountaintops to canyons below,
>   The river flows.

This mornin' she's a river running free,
Tomorrow she'll be looking to the sea,

Tomorrow she'll be gone a hundred miles,
Leaving nothing but the memory of her smile.

Moenkopi Memories

Moenkopi Memories surround the desert seeps,
Deep within the alcove ferns and sand,
The spirit of the Anasazi sleeps.
Beside a crumbling granary of stone and hand pressed clay,
The red sand ground is strewn with shards and flakes,
Reminders of a people gone away.

> Oh ancient ones ancestors what caused you to leave,
> Was it storm or was it famine or was it enemies?
> Ancient ones ancestors what made you travel on?
> Your culture and your people now
> Are scattered in Windsong.

Beneath a streaked and varnished sandstone wall
I seek some shade,
I see the pictographs and petroglyphs,
Signs of an artist's hand of a bygone age.
A broken pointed arrowhead dances in my mind,
Lying lost upon the dusty sands,
Where corn and plants and people lived and died.

Datura seeks the shadows and ravens touch the sky,
I stand inside a stone and cedar doorway,
To see the passing days through different eyes.
Lightning strikes the pinnacle I smell a desert rain,
The washes flash and fill with muddy soil,
And cut arroyo channels deep again.

Fire in the Sky

On the night the Aurora Borealis,
Reached out its northern lights,
And stretched its fiery fingers,
Across the southwest desert skies,
The wind blew in the canyons,
Shifting grains of sand,
Covering footsteps in time,
Made by a great man.

> Fire in the sky what do you know?
> Fire in the heart where did you go?
> May the long and lonely journey,
> Take Edward Abbey home.

One man with a vision,
One man with a dream,
One man with the power,
One man in between,
One to tell the world,
What it is about to lose,
One to keep the secrets,
From the money hungry fools.

Now a name lives on in solitude,
A name lives on in peace,
A name lives on in love for the desert,
For the sand wind rocks and trees,
And every time a coyote calls,
And vultures circle high,
We know that at great spirit,
Is somewhere still alive.

Wilderness Save Us (Direct Our Evolution)

The wilderness that once stood strong
Has now been taken by man.
The wild river's flow and places unknown
Have all been touched by human hands.

From the struggle to exist in a country untamed
Now only a memory survives,
But our spirit still retains a longing for the days
And places still untouched, free and wild.

> That call of the wild made humankind what it is,
> Without it alive we find that we cannot exist.
> We must direct our evolution
> To conserve the giving Earth with which we live,
> Preserve the wilderness for the vital life it gives.

The key to change is in our hands
And now must open the door.
Too many children and waste, greed and haste
Have made the human race weak and poor.

Respect for the land and things worked by hand
Will mark the steps to a new way.
Letting nature survive, preserve the last of the free and wild,
Begin this very moment, start today.

Great Massive Stone in the River

Tell me a story from a long time ago,
Draw me a picture with your hands.
Let my imagination take me far away
To unknown lands.

Sing me a song a hundred years old,
Accompanied by an instrument of wood.
Let melodies and voices carry harmonies
Which sound so good.

> And we'll let the future
> Fall away to the past,
> While we relive (old) traditions.
> Amidst the swift currents
> Of technology and change,
> We'll stand fast,
> Like a great massive stone in the river.

Give me night of soft warm candle light
And an hour of good conversations.
Let's talk of the great writers
Who have left their mark
And inspiration.

Play me a game of thinking skill and wit
While I sharpen my old intuition.
Let me feel the reassurance
Of being in control
Of my position.

Hand Made Time

I sat for a while in a big rocking chair
On an old plank porch with a wood railing,
My feet propped up, I drifted and dreamed
My thoughts on a summer wind sailin'

    Catching breezes and waves from a place far away
    And feeling a time that's gone by,
    A time when things moved at a much slower pace
    Like the stars slippin' through the night sky.

The old plank porch creaked as I lay back my head
And looked up at the handmade oak ceiling.
I could see callused hands as they'd plane and sand
'Till the wood was just right to the feeling.

    There was a time when they built things that way,
    But now it's a time that's gone by,
    A time when things moved at a much slower pace
    Like the stars moving through the night sky.

I walk from the place on ancient flagstones
Beneath two great hardwood trees,
And the moments I've spent contemplating the past
Have somehow brought new hope to me.

    Though I leave the dirt road
    For a fast-paced highway,
    An image remains in my mind,
    Of a time when things moved at a much slower pace,
    Like the stars slippin' through the night sky.
    Yes and sometimes I choose that much slower pace
    Like stars slippin' along through the night sky.

Ponderosa Sing to Me

I hear an old friend of mine in the whispering pines
Callin' me back to the warm sunshine,
Calling' me back to the rollin' foothills,
Where my wandering memories travel to still.

    Ponderosa sing in the wind,
    Take me, take me, take me back again,
    To the whispering pines in the summer time,
    And to you, my childhood friend.

We learned there to listen, to feel and to smell
The ways of the forest in the pine covered hills.
We learned there to wander and to talk to the trees,
In my heart the mountain woodlands still call to me.

    Ponderosa sing in the wind,
    Take me, take me, take me back again,
    To the whispering pines in the warm sunshine,
    And to you, my childhood friend.

Now I listen to stories and the winds in my mind,
And I think of your ways so gentle and kind.
To the sweet scents of a summer night I close my eyes
And dream we are walking once again through the pines.

Gold and Wood

A gold watch and a chain
And my grandpa's middle name
Go with me down the dusty roads of life.
The things he made of wood
And the words on which he stood
Will always keep a part of him alive.

While showin' me the needles and the leaves
Of the great northwestern trees
He compared the woods to people walking by.
He called each one by name
As the old trees creaked and swayed
And the breeze would carry back their soft reply.

> And he'd say,
> "Grandson when you grow as old
> As I am here right now,
> You'll see a lot you've meant to do
> Has passed you by somehow.
> But just believe you've learned a bit
> In everything you've done,
> And add it all up with a smile
> When you're old as I, Grandson."

His love was carved by hand
Through years of aging wood,
His hammer was the heartbeat of his life,
And as I use the tools that once were held by him
I sometimes feel him workin' by my side.

A gold watch tickin' still and the dreams I've yet to fill
Remind me of the sunshine in his eyes.

As the wind blows through the door
And sweeps the woodchips from the floor,
I know that part of Grandpa never died.

Song for the Burr Trail

There was a trail in Southeast Utah,
It was an old road travelin' into the wilderness.
It ran through, the heart of a desert
That was still untouched by the settling of the west.

But then the highways and growing towns drew closer,
The water rose and power crossed the land.
The old road was graded wider,
And an artery through the last frontier was planned.

> Now they want to carve an ugly scar
> Through the southeast wilderness,
> Grade and pave the old Burr Trail
> In the name of cash progress.
> But the people who have seen
> The beauty of the land as it now stands
> Will fight to save this last frontier
> From the highway builder's hands.

A coyote calls from up the silent canyon,
Cottonwood and juniper reply,
The painted rocks cool with the sunset,
The Earth would feel the loss if this place dies!

The old dirt road is still and peaceful,
A narrow trail winding in the night,
In a far off city, the battle quickens,
Will this wilderness survive 'till the morning light?

From the Mountains Down

Where the mountains touch the sky
A mighty river rollin' by,
Red sandstone canyons from the highlands tumble down,
About as far as you can be
From the cities or the seas,
That's where you'll find me, riding the desert breeze.

From the high LaSal on down to the Moab Valley,
The aspen share their space with the scrub oak tree,
With the Redtail Hawk and the Eagle on the wing,
The Canyon Wren makes the painted walls ring.

Where hearty souls before
Farmed the canyon floors,
And they made their homes in the high wall grottoes,
With the bluest skies around,
In the evening the stars shine down,
But you can see colors on the night of a big full moon.

White capped peaks framed in a window of red rock,
Snowmelt churns in the rapids of the wild Colorado,
You can see for miles from the top of a high plateau,
As the sunset lingers west in a fiery glow.

From the high LaSal on down to the Moab Valley,
With the pine and the fir and the sage and the juniper tree,
Redtail Hawk and the Eagle on the wing,
The Canyon Wren makes the painted walls sing.

Mountain Goats

Mountain Goats on a knife edge ridge
Standin' in the trail,
Mountain Goats on a knife edge ridge
Where the wild winds wail,
And the leader of the herd
Stands firmly facing strong,
Saying, "No I will not step aside
Until my family moves on."

        And the ways of the wild
        Sometimes stop us in our tracks;
        It's good to realize and feel
        When it's time to step back.

Lightning bolts strike on the peak
Thunder crashes down,
Flashing death and danger flies
Cold rain hits the ground,
And the cloud and the storm
Stand firmly facing strong,
"This mountaintop I claim as mine
'Till my cloud passes on."

Grizzly standing twelve feet tall
Investigates the trail,
Grizzly standing up ahead
You'd best turn your tail,
And the bear in the wilderness
Stands firmly facing strong,
"No I will not step aside
So you had best be gone.
This is where we all abide
And we must carry on."

Ranger's Call

Way up in the central Rockies
Where the Snake and the Teton flow,
In an undiscovered corner
Of the great Yellowstone,
Worked a ranger by the name of Dunbar
Who remains a legend still,
Building bridges cabins and trails,
Keepin' watch for the poacher's kill.
Where the pines make way for the meadows,
And the canyon firs grow tall
Along the Bechler River,
Where the Osprey fish the falls.

    Dunbar still calls to the wilderness,
    Calls to ranger's hearts who are the best,
    Calls to the rest of the world,
    To protect this National Park,
    Dunbar still calls to the wilderness.

Black Bear Moose and Grizzly,
Snd the Cranes fly with the Swans,
Where the big Elk call on the autumn winds
Snd the winter's deep and long,
I could imagine some of his stories
As I read old log books of ranger's lines,
How they'd work twelve hours,
Then chase a poacher into the night.
He must have inspired dedication
With an ethic of good hard work,
And yet there must have been much more to him
Than was left behind in words.

He was gone by the time that I worked those trails
But much of his work remained,
Though time and nature are claiming
Some of the fine things that he made.
But old ways give to new ones,
And few now understand
That the work done long before them
Was inspired by a love for the land.
But sometimes a true ranger
Will emerge with a passion strong
And be willing to listen to the ways of old,
Be willing to carry on.

> Where Dunbar still calls to the wilderness,
> Calls to ranger's hearts who are the best,
> Calls to the rest of the world,
> To protect this National Park,
> Dunbar still calls to the wilderness.

Summits That He Climbed

Johnny didn't fit into the four brick walls of school,
Ridiculed and rebellious, he was labeled as a fool.
Diagnosed and analyzed as a kid who could not learn,
He walked the lonely corridors afraid of every turn.

His family didn't understand his anger and his pain,
There never was a place for him, he just was not the same.
Every day he'd count the hours searching for a friend,
Loneliness in the empty faces, wishing for the day to end.

> But a night the coyote came to him
> And called him out to play,
> Introduced him to the raven
> And the windy canyon ways.
> The Bighorn of the mountain cliffs
> Watched as Johnny climbed,
> Always there to lead him on to s
> Summits of dreamtime.

One morning found him struggling once more with the law,
The iron hand of justice cut him down a swing he never saw,
Tight clasped grip now wrapped around the cold blue steel bars,
Bitter tears in a young man's eyes that were meant to see the stars.

Then a man named Mountain Jim sometimes known as Owl
Burned through Johnny's papers, took him from behind the bars.
He looked into the bottom depths of Johnny's lonely eyes,
Said, "For the next six weeks, Kid, you're going to learn to climb."

Johnny turned his life around from the mountain side,
Learned to make the pieces fit from the summits that he climbed.
They now call him J.K. Bighorn when he visits school,

Looking with an Eagle Eye for kids labeled as fools.

> For long ago the coyote came to him
> And called him out to play,
> Introduced him to the raven
> And the windy canyon ways.
> The Bighorn of the mountain cliffs
> Taught Johnny how climbed,
> Always there to lead him on to s
> Summits of dreamtime.
> Now he's always there to bring new blood
> Onto the mountainside.

Heart of the Desert

In the heart of the desert I will walk,
In the heart of the middle of the land of the high plateau,
In the heart of the desert I will walk,
In the heart of the middle of the canyons of the high plateau.

In the heart where the sun shines bright,
Of the desert stars at night,
Are jewels scattered in a velvet sky.
In the heart where the high rock walls,
Of the desert standing tall,
Remind me of the endless age of time.

In the heart where the river flows,
Of the desert down below,
Are places lying hidden and still unknown.
In the heart where I know that a dream,
Of the desert still is real,
And I'll keep it livin' for the world to know.

Old Dusty Road

An old dusty road, tennis shoe walkin'
Thinkin' and talkin' again.
A long fence post row, barbed wire all saggin'
Something's a naggin' my brain.
Ditch water flows, creek is still rollin'
Down from the mountain to the plain.

> As we walk along
> Suddenly it strikes me,
> That we're turning history's pages
> With the steppin' of our feet.
> For as long as there's still dirt
> To be kicked up on some old dirt track,
> We can find the place we went awry;
> We can find our way back.

An old mining trail, hiking boot walkin'
Thinkin' and talkin' again.
Tailings are spilled, mountainside flaggin'
Something's a naggin' my brain.
Rusty iron rail, clings to the Cliffside,
Still gold and silver in the vein.

Shady country lane, soft sandal walkin
Thinkin' and talkin' again.
Great trees in line, old limbs arch over,
Something's a naggin' my brain.
Foundation stone, fireplace still standin'
Hand hewn to last and to remain.

I Am The Wind

I'm the breeze that carries scents,
Of the early rain on sage,
Across the rocks and sand
Of the desert plain.
I'm the wind that shapes the clouds,
In the ever-changing skies,
Where high mountain peaks and eagles,
And the sun and moon reside.
I'm the blow that brings the storm,
Between the lightning and the rain
And whips the mighty waters,
Of the ocean seas and lakes.

I am the wind I am the gale
I am the breeze that fills the sails,
I am the gust I am the cyclone,
I'm squall that brings the storm,
I am the zephyr, on a windy morn.
No-one knows where I begin,
Or when someday I'll end,
Across the sea out from the mountains,
Before me you will bend,
I am the wind. I am the wind.

On my current travels those with wings,
I move across the planet,
In my pathways seasons lie,
And the moisture of the lands.
Some know me as Aeolus,
Tornado Typhoon Drift,
Some know me as Hurricane,
Simoom or Tempest,

Some call me Monsoon Cyclone Blizzard
Sirocco Tramontane,
But to the Earth I'm all one in the same-I am the wind.

Seasons Are Changin'

      Seasons are changin', all rearrangin'
      Getting' ready for something new to come in.
      Old leaves are dying, birds are all a flyin',
      You can feel it in the wind.

Soon the snows of winter must fall,
So the spring can come again.
In the memory of summer sun now gone,
Seeds are planted deep within.

Late in the winter, hear the lonely call
Echo from the mountains high and white.
From somewhere hidden deep within the melting snow
Will come the first new signs of life.

So the circle of life continues on,
Everything must die to live once again.
To hear the rhythm of the seasons turning 'round,
Just listen to the wind.

Drinkin' From a Glass

I'm drinkin' from a glass that once was a jar,
It came to the grocery full of salsa from a garden farm.
As I quench my thirst from this jar of mine,
I think of the factory that made this glass so fine,

> So recycle replace reuse and retrace,
> It will save the mountains trees forests seas and lakes,
> Recycle replace reuse and retrace,
> If we take some careful steps it will not be too late.

My tools are in a metal box that once was a car,
It drove a hundred thousand miles straight to the junkyard.
As I finish work and I put my tools away,
I think of the salvage work that uses cars again.

My bicycle's recycled from aluminum,
My rollerblades are made from remelted plastic gum.
As I roll through life on my spinning wheels,
I think of what I'm saving and how good it feels.

Last Night the Old Arch Tumbled Down

Last night the old arch tumbled down
With no-one but coyotes to hear the sound
Of the old weathered sandstone
As it fell to the ground.

And in the morning a park ranger found,
That the trail was rerouted where the deer walked around,
Where last night in the moonlight
The old arch tumbled down.

> But the people, cried sadly,
> And the newspaper mourned,
> That the saddest time ever to come to this town
> Was the night the old arch tumbled down.

Near dawn of the night it fell down
It echoed through canyons, a shock wave of sound,
Saying goodbye to ten thousand years
It stood o'er the ground.

In the morning a hawk felt a roar
Of a rumbling of sandstone so he turned and he soared
Flying up past the cliffside
Where the arch stood no more.

> And still the people,
> All cried sadly, and the newspapers bemoaned,
> That worst type of disaster to come to this town
> Was the night the old arch tumbled down.

Last night, indeed, the arch tumbled down,
With no-one but a bunch of carefree coyotes

To listen to the sound,
Of the old weathered sandstone as it fell to the ground.

And in the morning a patrolling park ranger found,
That the trail had simply been rerouted
Where the sensible deer walked around
The rubble of the arch as it lay on the ground,
For last night in the moonlight
The old arch tumbled down.

Save The Canyon Wilderness

Go ahead and grade and pave the last enchanted trails,
Dump wastes upon the desert until the clear skies pale,
Then watch the dying eagles as they fall from the sky,
Bringing us together as we hear their final cries.

   For you've given us a reason to rise again and stand
   You threaten our freedom and destroy desert land.
   You've given us a cause to join our strength as one,
   We'll save the canyon wilderness; the time to fight has come.

You say we're just a minority with an environmental craze,
But you don't see yet how many have walked the desert ways.
The healing from this country is like a gift of life,
And those who have received it will never let it die.

Some will fight with politics, some will fight with song.
Some will use the written word, the rest will come along.
A wave will wash the high desert sands,
And sweep them clear of destructive plans.

Carry Me Across The Canyon

Carry me across the canyon,,
Where the Lone Pinyon grows,
Carry me across the canyon,
To a place that nobody knows.

There I'll fly with the Eagle,
There I'll drift down below.
Carry me across the canyon,
To a place that nobody knows.

Let me walk in the desert,
With the sage, wind and sand,
Let me walk in the desert,
Feel the touch of her hand.

Let me flow with the river,
Let me tumble and roll,
Let me flow with the river,
Ever changing I go.

About the Author

Mark Doherty spent the first twenty-seven years of his life growing up in and roaming the foothills of the Rocky Mountains outside of Boulder Colorado. The next thirty-three years found him wandering the Utah deserts and mountains. He began writing poems and songs inspired by nature in his early teens and has never stopped. Meanwhile, Doherty worked his way through the West employed at variety of jobs including backcountry guide, musician, carpenter, water commissioner, ski patrolman, journalist and freelance writer.

Between his wanderings and work, he acquired his BA in English from Western State University in Gunnison Colorado and his teaching certificate from Mesa State University in Grand Junction and Westminster College in Salt Lake City. At 33, he married mountaineer and outdoorswoman Deborah Read and began his career as an English Teacher in the high school setting.

While teaching, Doherty not only continued to write poetry, but he also penned two novellas, two poetry volumes, one short story volume, and two book length volumes of essays--the most recent essay volume is set for publication by Unsolicited Press in August of 2020.

In 2016, Doherty earned his masters degree in Creative Writing Nonfiction from Southern New Hampshire University. He currently teaches English 11 and International Baccalaureate English at Hillcrest High School in Midvale, Utah. Whenever possible, he and his wife travel the mountains, deserts, rivers and waterways of the West.

Visit Mark's website www.moenkopimemories.org to follow his writing journey and for links to audio recordings of many of the lyrical poems in this chapbook.

www.ingramcontent.com/pod-product-compliance
Lightning Source LLC
Chambersburg PA
CBHW071751080526
44588CB00013B/2211